Alistair Bryce-Clegg

EARLY YEARS
DISPLAY

How to make your display child-led and child-centred

Featherstone Education
An imprint of Bloomsbury Publishing Plc

50 Bedford Square
London
WC1B 3DP
UK

1385 Broadway
New York
NY 10018
USA

www.bloomsbury.com

FEATHERSTONE and the Feather logo are trademarks of Bloomsbury Publishing Plc

First published in Great Britain 2014

A catalogue record for this book is available from the British Library.

ISBN
PB: 9781408155486

4 6 8 10 9 7 5

Typeset by Newgen Knowledge Works (P) Ltd., Chennai, India
Printed and bound in India by Replika Press Pvt. Ltd

This book is produced using paper that is made from wood grown in managed, sustainable forests.
It is natural, renewable and recyclable. The logging and manufacturing processes conform
to the environmental regulations of the country of origin.

To find out more about our authors and books visit www.bloomsbury.com.
Here you will find extracts, author interviews, details of forthcoming events
and the option to sign up for our newsletters.

Thank you to all the children and practitioners whose images
appear in this book with special mention to:
Fee Bryce-Clegg, Jill Hutton, Middlefield Primary School, Kids Allowed Nursery, Dee Point
Primary School, St Andrew's Primary School, The Friars Primary School, Halton Lodge
Primary, Ladybrook Primary School, St Thomas More C of E Primary, Haven Nursery School,
St Francis Primary School, Acorn Childcare Ltd and the London Early Years Foundation.

Special thanks also to TTS who provided many of the resources used in the photographs.

Contents

Preface

ABC says

My first ever teaching practice disaster involved a Rapunzel display, some boys, a vast quantity of brown paint and a pair of cream linen trousers!

It was the sort of display that was very fashionable in the early 1990s and formed the basis of most of the display that I produced in my early teaching career. I think it was commonly known as a 'frieze' where an adult would decide what the board was going to look like and then give the children activities, that weren't necessarily linked to learning, but done to produce the various elements that were needed to make the frieze look good. As I remember, this one needed lots of car sponges, paper plates and yellow wool....

Where to start? Well, I am the son of a teacher and as such had spent a great deal of my youth either at my own school or in my mum's school, and if we weren't actually in the building, we seemed to be doing something related to it. So, I knew from an early age that other than being a Blue Peter presenter, teaching is what I wanted to do. Now as my mum was a 'junior' teacher her entire Primary School career, it was juniors that I wanted to teach. I might have gone to 'top infants' at a push, but certainly nothing below that.

I announced this fact with great conviction to my University tutor who, with a wise eye and slightly sarcastic tone, explained that I had signed up to a Primary teaching course, therefore I would need to experience the primary age range.

My anguished pleas of not wanting to spend my career 'wiping other people's children's bottoms' and 'reading stories' all day apparently fell on deaf ears as my very first teacher training placement was in Reception. Reception! It couldn't have been worse. I wasn't best pleased, and vowed to get through it as quickly and painlessly as possible.

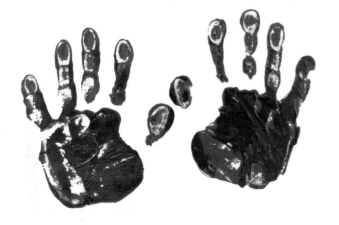

When the day to begin the placement came, my only real dilemma was what to wear. It was an unusually hot September and I decided that cream linen was the way forward (as you do!) so that is what I wore.

I arrived and was introduced to the class teacher Sally who (once she had looked in disbelief at my legware) asked me if I had ever taught in Reception before. I replied 'no' and that is where I should have left it. But such was my distain at being placed with this age group that I couldn't resist adding 'but how hard can it be?'. I think at that moment Sally decided to show me just how hard it could be. How do you teach a cocky young student a lesson he will never forget? With the help of a Rapunzel display, some wall paper, several car sponges and a tray of brown paint.

If memory serves me right, the 'topic' was 'Story book' and the focus for this week's story was Rapunzel. Rapunzel herself, or at least her head, had already been made out of a paper plate and lots of yellow wool. All she needed was a tower to hang her hair out of. Seemingly as a result of my barbed comment, that creation of the tower was to be my job. I had clear instructions: take the children outside and look at the brickwork on the walls of the school, then take a rubbing. Come back in and using the car sponges and the brown paint, recreate the pattern on the back of a roll of wallpaper. This was sounding very simple. That was until I met my group of children. There were eight of them, all boys, I suspect hand picked for their lack of attention and non compliance – well, that is what you get for being cocky!

Once I had got their attention (for all of 30 seconds) off I went, doing my 'junior' teacher bit. It didn't go well! We never actually made it outside to look at the brickwork. In fact, I didn't even get to the end of my explanation! As soon as they saw the sponges and the paint, they were off – literally.

There was one who turned out to be the ringleader. He looked at the sponges and then looked at me. Without shifting his gaze from mine, he slowly lowered himself down and picked up a sponge. As soon as he had one in his hand, they all followed suit. My pleas to stop fell on deaf ears. Before I knew it, not only did they all have a sponge, the sponges were in the paint. Little hands were now agitating and squeezing their sponges so that the paint began to bubble and run down their hands and onto their uniform.

Then the first 'splat' happened. Big and messy, right in the middle of the wallpaper. If that wan't bad enough, it was followed by a slide. Like one giant poo stripe right up Rapunzel's tower! I tried everything I knew, pleading, threatening, negotiating…but the lure of the paint and the sponges was too strong. These boys were having a giddy old time.

Then it happened. That voice. Clear, strong and commanding. Two words was all it took to bring this disaster to an end. Two words that I must have said a thousand times to these boys with no effect, but when Sally said them they worked. 'Stop it!'. These were quickly followed with another two words, Stand up!'. The first two had been almost bellowed, but these ones were in a very low, slow (and slightly sinister) voice. It was then that I found myself in a line up of four year olds. Eyes down, paint dripping off the ends of our fingers, all of us aware of how much trouble we were about to be in.

At this point you would imagine that I was thinking that perhaps my teaching career was over, that I had brought shame upon myself and my professional credibility – but you would be wrong. As my head hung in shame I only had one thought: 'Theses trousers are dry clean only!'. Worse than that, because it was brown paint, I looked like I had had a very unfortunate accident of my own!

Sally was not happy. She told us to go to the toilets and get cleaned up. In one more unbelievable lack of foresight and experience, the children went to their toilet and I went to the staff toilet, spending a good five minutes splashing copious amounts of water onto my trousers and attempting to dry them off under the hand drier.

Needless to say, when I got back all was not well. My Reception boys had also had a whale of a time in the toilets and re-enacted their painting escapades only this time with brown soap streaks all over the mirrors. They had also managed to fill every sink and print a brown hand print onto every available surface.

I spent the remainder of the morning cleaning the boys' toilets before a severe lunch time dressing down. When I look back it is amazing that I was allowed to come back the next day, but come back I did. By the end of my placement I had completely fallen for the Early Years and never really left. As for Rapunzel, she got her tower following a more successful second attempt with a group of far more compliant children and a more considered wardrobe choice!

Introduction

I think where we practitioners can sometimes go wrong with display is being clear about what the 'something' is that we are displaying, and why we are displaying it in the first place! Indeed, we should not be giving children work in order to create a display – instead we should display the work that they have created using the processes we have taught them.

When I first started teaching, display was something that you tended to do en masse to make your space look attractive. It was done exclusively by adults and how good your displays were directly reflected on how good a practitioner you were.

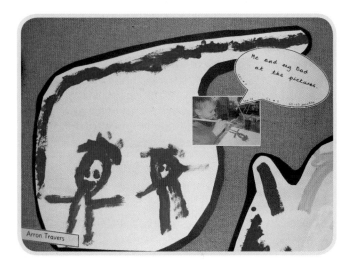

In the early 1990s it was all about the drapes: every display had to have at least one drape in a coordinating colour. Fail to drape in a display, and your display failed! Displays were always linked to the current topic. You would plan them in advance and then you would give children activities to create a display, regardless of assessment or links to learning. I remember creating a jungle role-play area once and spending many afternoons getting the children to sponge print with shades of green onto large pre-cut leaves. I also got them to stick scrunched-up tissue paper balls into the outline of a chimpanzee, and some poor children spent their time stuffing 'American Tan' tights with newspaper and then painting them green for creepers (I have not seen such an effective use of a reinforced gusset either before or since!).

When I look back now, all of those activities had a very low skill level and a very high boredom threshold, yet that is what we did for our displays. The truth is that even though that was a good 20 years ago now, I still see lots of elements of that sort of practice in settings today.

What is display for?

In the style of … syndrome

Many teachers encourage children to all create similar pieces of artwork, 'in the style of' a famous artist. For this approach, think 'skill' rather than 'activity'. I remember my first 'in the style of' experience. It was in a large primary school in Manchester, I was teaching reception, and the planning called for us to 'paint in the style of Van Gogh', using 'Sunflowers' as a reference. I loved it! The finished display took us about a week to create. I decided that we weren't going to do a Van Gogh copy each, we were going to create a giant sized version of the picture that would fill the huge display board next to my blackboard (blackboard! that tells you how long ago it was, we didn't even have a computer in the classroom let alone an ICT suite!).

During lunch time I would set up the classroom for 'painting'. I mixed all of the paints, matching them to the colours on my poster. I then added flour (for thickness) and PVA glue for the 'sheen' of oil paint. I grouped the children on tables (sitting down) and each group had one of the flower heads to reproduce. When I say reproduce, I don't mean interpret, I mean reproduce (almost to the brush stroke).

I spent my time moving between the tables, enthusing, encouraging and 'adjusting' the work that children had produced, 'enhancing' their artistry with a tweak here and an addition there. Until, finally it was done.

The reason I remember this display so well is that other adults in the school loved it. It got me high levels of praise all round and even the junior staff were sent down to look at it (I know, even the juniors!). It got me so much kudos that I had a flash of inspiration – an idea that really showed off my inventive and creative streak. I would do the display again for the other side of my blackboard, only this time I wouldn't do sunflowers, I would do moonflowers. I think I made some tenuous link in my planning to hot and cold colours and before you could say 'death by disengagement', we were off! Because the sunflowers had been so well received, the pressure was on to make this one just as good. As a result the children got even less freedom than they had the first time round. One heavily directed week later, there it was, and here it is …

So thrilled was I with what I had done that I took photos and kept them! So thrilled were the school that I was asked by the head if I would take it down and put it up again in the entrance hall, then everyone who visited the school would see it. I had arrived!

WRONG APPROACH

This story is an example of how I think display has lost its way. Surely everything we do with children is about expanding their knowledge, skills and experiences. We are encouraging them to be creative and unique, not to be carbon copies of someone else. Also, our walls are part of our learning space and should be there to support and celebrate teaching and learning, and not just look pretty.

The main issue with effective display is adults (like me) who celebrate the coordination, colour and 'prettiness' of what is on the walls and don't question the skill, learning and engagement that went into creating it. Display doesn't have to be dull, but it should be meaningful, relevant and full of learning.

I am not saying no one should ever look at Van Gogh's 'Sunflowers' in the classroom ever again, but rather than everyone painting a sunflower, teach the children a skill using Van Gogh as an inspiration. If they don't paint a sunflower, does it matter? I would say the answer is 'No! Absolutely not!'.

I think that good early years teaching should always focus on what the children are learning from the 'process' rather than just planning for the outcome; and as your display is part of your learning environment, I think a good display can reflect skill differentiation and attainment as well. I will investigate this idea further and show you some examples later on in the book.

I ranted about my Van Gogh experience on my blog at the time and am still ranting now! (See opposite).

ABC DOES...

search

TWITTER

FACEBOOK

Categories

ARCHIVES

Now, don't get me wrong. I like Van Gogh. If you are going to 'do' a painter he has to have something for everyone. Don't forget, there are some children who will visibly wilt at the sight of a vase full of yellow flowers. If you are thinking about trying to get high levels of engagement then flowers don't always do it! But, Van Gogh came up trumps due to the fact that he was a little unhinged and chopped off his own ear (now that is more like it)! Better than that, he then painted a picture of himself in a rather fetching bandage ...

When we look at the 'style' of an artist that is exactly what we should be teaching. What techniques did Van Gogh use that made lots of his pictures have the same feel even though the content and colours were often different?

In essence for me, it comes down to 'very thick paint' and using something other than a brush – fingers, a play dough tool, or a kitchen spatula. I am sure Van Gogh didn't use a kitchen spatula but the whole point is that we don't want children to paint exactly like Van Gogh – we are looking at style.

Like everything else in the early years it should be about teaching children a PROCESS that they don't associate with one thing but can creatively apply to many situations. You should NOT get all of the children to produce a version of 'Sunflowers' because the learning outcome was not 'to accurately produce a copy of a great masterpiece'! By saying to children that they must all produce a version of Van Gogh's painting, you are setting them up to fail and closing down any chance of them expressing their own creativity.

You need to identify the 'technique', or 'process', and let the children experiment with it, producing any sort of picture they want to. You should not give children work to create a display, you should display the work that they create using the processes you have taught them.

So... if you have sunflowers in your setting and you look at their sheer gorgeousness, you might well talk to the children about this bloke who is famous for painting pictures (and cutting off his ear). I would show them his painting of sunflowers and a VARIETY of his other work. Tell them that he used oil paints which are thick and shiny. Enthuse over how fantastically squidgy thick shiny paint feels, especially when you apply it with your fingers!

Then show the children how to add flour to ready-mix paint to really thicken it up and some PVA to make it shiny when it has dried (just like oil paint). Give them the paint and the flour and the glue and let them go for it! Then your display will not be 30 versions of 'Sunflowers' by Van Gogh but paintings using thick paint inspired by the work of Van Gogh. Of course once you have opened children's minds to the possibilities of thick paint you would then need to make the opportunity available for them to make their own, whenever they were inspired to do so.

When we teach children a new skill we then want them to be able to apply it to a variety of situations and not think that you can only use thick paint if you are painting sunflowers with a bandage over your ear!

Preparing for display

There is one thing display shouldn't be, and that is wallpaper! Instead, it needs to be meaningful for children and it can then play an important part in the learning process. To make a display meaningful to children, they have to be involved in its creation or appreciate the relevance of it.

That is why, for the beginning of the school year I would suggest that your walls are blank. They can be backed and bordered, but otherwise they should be empty. True blank canvasses for the children to fill.

I appreciate for some people the thought of doing this would be a huge leap of faith, but trust me, it is worth it in the long run. If you have a display that is already up when the children come in to your setting then they will all notice it, but only a small number will really see it. Of that small number very few, if any, will go on seeing it and then using it to support their learning. It is not that it's a magic display that can disappear,

or that the children go blind! It just becomes very familiar – literally 'the wallpaper' – and because they were not part of creating it and it isn't relevant to their learning, they just don't engage with it.

I have never worked with a setting yet where the children have come in and seen empty display boards and then called for 'more colour' or 'more display' before they can begin their learning!

I have, however, come across a number of adults who really struggle with the 'emptiness' and feel that it is a poor reflection on their practice or their setting. The truth is that within a very short space of time your boards are going to be overflowing with quality display linked to learning. I would rather wait and have that than a mass produced alphabet poster that no one looks at.

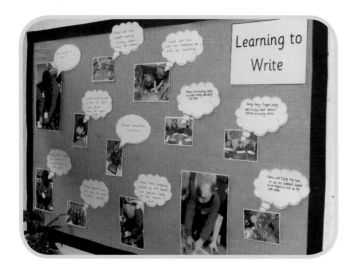

Backing your boards

So, if we are going to strip all our boards and back them in preparation for our new cohort, what should these boards look like?

In my day, I was the king of the contrasting backing and border. There was no combination too bold for me to try. Every board had a different coloured backing paper and often a number of colours in the border. I have backed in wrapping paper, foil, newsprint, wallpaper, print and collage. I have bordered with fairy lights, tinsel, leopard print, sweets and every mass produced border roll there was going. Once when I had finished, my classroom had the resemblance of a cross between Santa's grotto and a cheap brothel!

But, do you know what? I loved it, my headteacher loved it and parents loved it. They loved it because it was bright (very bright), cheerful and busy. All of the things that children like. Only, this was a learning environment that was supposed to support, not distract children on their learning journey. Being children, they didn't have the same experience, visual perception or misconceptions that the adults have. It is not the displays that make an inspiring or outstanding teacher. It is their ethos and understanding about child development which is why those displays eventually had to go (but not until I had used every last Fandango feather out of the stockroom!).

Your display should be there to help, inspire and promote children's learning. So, what is featured on that display needs to be relevant, purposeful and accessible to the children. They need to engage with it, understand it and then use it in their everyday learning.

Even though when they first walk into your space after you have been 'creative' with a display they will 'ooh' and 'ahhh' at the fact it has changed and that it is bright and colourful, the novelty will wear off and they will stop looking because it isn't relevant.

If they have produced a brilliant piece of mark-making and you have backed it in pink and orange and stuck it on a gold foil board with a glitter border, they will cease to see it because it will be lost amongst the brightness and the bling.

Evidence of early years children

In an early years environment that has really good display, I should be able to stand in the middle of the room, having not spoken to an adult or a child, not looked at a planning file or observation, and I should get a strong sense of the children who occupy the space. I should be able to see evidence of their voices having an impact on their environment, their personal preferences shaping the learning and their self esteem being raised by seeing photos of their achievements everywhere.

If I stand in the middle of a space and face a wall full of computer generated, downloaded laminates (however pretty they look to adults) I could be in anyone's space, anywhere. It may be bright and the walls may be festooned – but for children it is dull and lacks any sense of motivation or impact.

Children need to be able to identify their own work within a display. This visual stimulus will remind their brain of what it was they were doing when they created that piece of work; it will also remind them how happy you were when they had finished it, and how proud they were when you put it on the wall. This will then inspire them to apply their knowledge or skill that they used to other tasks that they do. Hence your display is having a direct impact on attainment.

But first, each child needs to see their work. Have it leap out as the most important thing on that board. Make it easy for their young, developing brain to be able to discriminate within what they are seeing.

KEEP IT NEUTRAL

For that to happen, your boards need to be neutral, I would go as far as to say beige! A common problem for settings that try the 'neutral' approach is that they go from being bright and cheery to being beige and boring.

In this two-form entry reception class they have used a completely monochrome approach to their point of entry display. I have to say that I really liked it. Not just because of the individuality that was evident, but because of the fact that it had clear links to assessment, physical development and attainment. Not to mention the fact that it looked great! All of the display boards were full of it. It is quite hard to capture the impact in one photo.

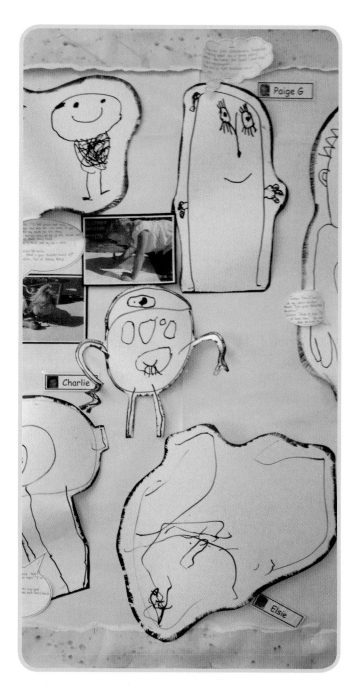

The assessment focus that had generated the images for the display was around the children's grip and fine and gross motor movement.

Not only could you see the stages of development in the size and content of the drawings themselves, but the comments and photographs that had been added gave the pictures context and showed that the staff were clear about the next developmental steps.

You can see from the photographs below that both the indoor and the outdoor environment was used to get high level engagement. In addition, a variety of sizes of paper and types of drawing material were matched to children's gross or fine motor dexterity. The fact that the photographs had been printed in black and white was a nice touch and helped give the display real impact. I think the key phrase to remember here is 'less is more, not less is morgue'.

Mood boards

Early years should be an exciting place to play and learn and display should be a reflection of that. But the energy and 'wow' factor should come from the content not the dressing, otherwise as my 94-year-old granny would say, 'It's all fur coat and no knickers'! If we are ditching the fur coat then we don't just want to be left with knickers, we want industrial, hold you in, push-you-up type control pants, that not only do a brilliant job, but also make you look like a million dollars! I think I might now be encouraging you to think about your displays as underwear which is not quite what I intended, but you get the idea!

A really useful exercise that I have done with a number of settings who were thinking about stripping back, is to create a mood board. You are not saying that 'we will only ever use the colours and patterns that we put on this board', but it gives the team lots to talk about in terms of why you have decided to strip things back and it also makes sure that everyone understands not only the concept, but also the 'feel' (oh, no – I have begun to sound like an interior designer)!

A mood board is basically a large(ish) board (I usually make mine A1 size) on which the team stick images, ideas, textures, colours, fabric etc. that they think encapsulate the feel of the environment, the sort of display you might have and a rough pallet of colours that you might use. Are you going natural or neon? Things like that.

Encourage all the staff to get involved and contribute so, over a period of time, people can add more to it once they get the idea. What is more important is that the things that you stick on it are the concepts behind 'why'. If the team don't get that, then you will be back to 'poncho pink' and 'purple haze' before you know it.

Here are a few tips for mood board making:

* Discuss the theory with the team first.

* Just because it was your idea don't come to the first meeting with enough 'stuff' to fill the board – it needs to be a shared ethos, not a dictatorship!

* Use real objects (3D objects like pine cones can be tricky to stick to the board but you can always display them tastefully around the bottom when you have finished).

* Use magazine cuttings, not just education catalogues.

* Use fabric, wool, thread, colour charts, photographs – anything that promotes discussion.

* Dig out some old wallpaper sample books and look for colour and texture in those.

* Don't just use search engine images, search more widely.

* Use a camera/phone to take pictures of parts of your exiting building and outdoor environment for inspiration. This could be part of a brick, some print, or a colour combination that you think works well.

* Use some text on your board. This can be a mixture of 'inspiration' texts, but also print that is clear and effective.

* Stick on examples of other displays that you have seen and liked. These can be from other settings but they could also be art displays, posters, anything really.

Once your mood board is complete you can then use it as a guide to the sorts of colours, themes and approaches that you want to use in your displays. Remember they are a starting point and not the law!

If you do decide to go for a more neutral background, there are lots of simple things that you can do to stop your displays from becoming insipid and dull. Here are some ideas using various other natural materials to pick out accent colours or create interesting borders.

Here, hessian makes a great background to this more ornate frame. It was part of a collection of different frames (without glass) that had a permanent home on the wall. Staff just changed the pictures that went in them.

Don't be afraid of a bit of 3D. Tactile resources can really lift a display and give it some interest.

Here the same idea was re-interpreted with pasta frames. Unless you could find a really good and convincing learning objective to attach to a mass frame making activity, the frames would be made by adults for impact!

Considering the gender of your display

One point that is worth considering when you have finished your board is how the environment you have created will impact on gender. Some boys' aversion to all things pink is not a conscious thought process, but an ingrained learned response to gender roles that have been passed onto them. Usually these are well established by the time a child is about two-years-old. So, when you are thinking about your display, make sure that your backgrounds are neutral but also that they do not cater too much for the preferences of one particular group of children.

The game that I like to play with settings is 'If you had to give 'it' a gender, what gender would you give it?' The 'it' can be any aspect of your environment or provision, but in this case we are talking about display. If the answer to your question is clearly 'male' or 'female' then your dressing is not neutral enough. This should always be the case unless you have specifically dressed an area or a resource around the interests of a particular group of children.

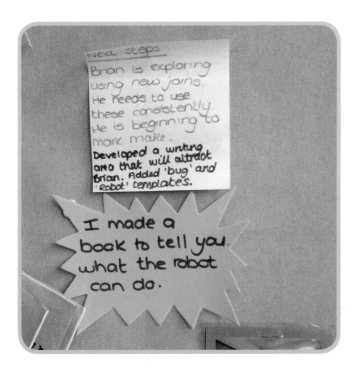

Bear in mind that gender is not the same as sex. The World Health Organisation says that:

Gender is the characteristics, roles and responsibilities of women and men, boys and girls, which are socially constructed. Gender is related to how we are perceived and expected to think and act as women and men because of the way society is organised, not because of our biological differences.

So, it is possible to give the spaces that we create a gender whilst not necessarily intending them to be for 'boys' or 'girls'. One of the issues that often arises in early years spaces is that because they are predominantly created by humans with a strong female gender imprint, they can then appear very feminine to children who have a more culturally stereotypically masculine gender.

Gender stereotyping is a complex and subtle thing and most children have got a very strong gender imprint by the time that they are two. The socially accepted view of the gender that has been attached to their biological state will have been thrust upon them from the moment they were born, from the colour of the babygro we put them in to the type of language and cultural references that we use about and to them.

ABC says

When we are thinking about the environments and displays that we create and how they appear to all children, then all of that gender stereotyping and conformity comes into play. Not all of the time with every child, but most of the time with most children.

Display and print

You need to consider if your display is 'print rich' or just full of print. 'Print rich' is a lovely phrase, but it is one that is easily misinterpreted and can cause practitioners a great deal of angst, not to mention headaches for children! So, what is a print rich environment? Well, for me the most important word in the phrase is not 'print', it is 'rich'. If we think about the word 'rich' in monetary terms, it just means that you have got a lot of it. But when it comes to learning through print, less is often more – at least to start with.

This, for example, is a very busy space. For me, any one aspect of it is lost in the sheer explosion of text. Although there is a lot of information, it would be very difficult for the emergent learner to unpick and apply it.

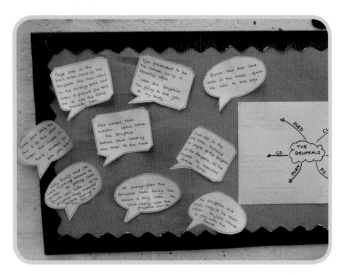

Print in your environment is only 'rich' for children if they are interested in it and engage with it. If there is lots of it then it just becomes wallpaper. At the early stages of development, when children are recognising different letter and number shapes, print doesn't only just need to be engaging, it needs to be clear. To an 'emerging eye', a, o, b, d, c, p, q, e and g can look very similar to each other. So if they are displayed all in the same font and colour within a very busy background then the chances are they won't be as engaging to young children.

If we use print in the environment to teach children that print carries meaning, then it makes sense for children to be involved in the creation of that print. This could be labels for the classroom or on a display. Recording in display what the children say about their work or what they think about what they have been doing, along with their photographs, can be a great way of getting them to engage with the print that is on the walls.

I would say that there also needs to be a variety of styles of print mixed in with adults and children's mark-making and writing that has been done 'live' in the setting.

The main body of print on your walls should be meaningful and relevant to the children and produced by an adult or child working in the space. Then enhancements to your printed environment can be made using other examples and styles of print. But you should view this sort of print in the same way as you do an enhancement to any part of your provision as just that, an enhancement.

PURPOSE OF LABELLING

Consider the purpose of this type of display in a water area for non-reading early years children? Do we have it because it is a well known fact that children don't know how to play with water unless there are a few blue circles next to them with text they can't read in it? Even if you can read it – is it ever going to influence their play?

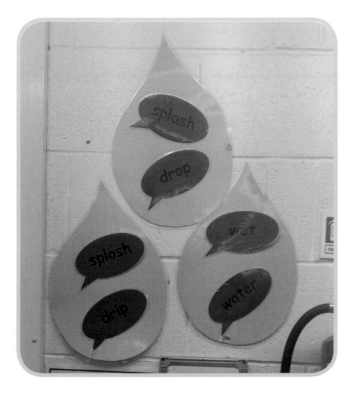

It can be a really good idea to have labels near to provision to help, support and focus children's learning, but only if they can actually engage with the print. A good idea is to use the children themselves to make the labels. Then you can talk about ideas and expectations while they are making them and the children will have a memory prompt when they look at them.

If in doubt, do the squint test. Stand about six feet away from your board and squint at it. If the children's work is the background, and the border and the labelling all merge into one riot of colour and pattern, then you have got it wrong. If the children's work 'pings' out at you (and them), then you have got it right. After all, what is display for? It is there to motivate children by raising their self esteem or to teach them something that they need to know. It is not about making wallpaper.

ABC says

There will be lots and lots of other opportunities for you to introduce print into your environment through books, comics, letters etc. Just make sure your walls are print rich and not just full of print.

Displays to teach, celebrate and document

ABC says

So, once you have sorted out how your displays might look, then you need to work out what you are going to put on them. A good display can have many purposes, but they should all be linked to learning in some way, shape or form.

For me, display tends to fall into three broad categories:

✔ **teach and inspire**

✔ **celebrate**

✔ **document**

I would list them in that order of importance and prominence within your environment.

25.1.13
We warmed up with some delicious hot chocolate around the fire circle.

Display to teach and inspire

If I said that I would start by linking your display to assessment, it all begins to sound a little bit (well, very) dry and dull. But, the use of assessment and observation is crucial when you are planning next steps for children and if you want your display to show learning and differentiation, then it needs to be linked to your assessments. We don't often think about a display being able to teach, but really, that should be one of its primary functions. But to teach successfully, you need to engage and that can be where some displays fall down.

To engage you have to be visible. I am not going to interact with something that I can't see or access. So, the ideal height for your teaching display is child eye level. As human beings we look ahead and down most of the time. This is how nature made us, so that we could scan the horizon for predators and prey and also look for food, resources (and big holes that we might fall into) on the ground. We had very few predators from above and few resources and food sources, therefore we don't really look up unless prompted to do so.

The further up the wall your display is, the less impact it will have for children without direction to it. This also applies when we are hanging copious amounts of 'stuff' from the ceiling, on hula hoops, washing lines and bits of string! Ask yourself the question, who looks at it? Also, what impact does it have on teaching and learning, and how does it impact on cluttering my space?

FROM A CHILD'S POINT OF VIEW

Say, for example, you have a water tray indoors. Above your water tray you have a lovely umbrella and from that umbrella you have laboriously laminated and cut out loads of raindrops on which are printed adjectives that relate to water. It has taken you ages to hang them from the edges of your brolly and you get really annoyed when the door to outside is opened and they all blow about and tangle with each other!

The question is the same as always *'Who is this display for?'*. **Is it for children? How many children ever approached a water tray and said 'Now, before we start engaging in water play, let's just cast our eyes in a heavenly direction and reflect on some of these appropriately placed adjectives that link to water play.'?** The answer is none – ever!

Does it really make it a print rich space, when the drops are all the same size and same colour and printed in the same font and twirling round in the breeze? No! So, what is it for? Even though I have created many versions of this sort of display in my time for 'children', the answer is that this sort of display is for adults, because we like it, it looks coordinated and attractive, and we can make the link between adjectives and learning. But children just don't.

As adults, our brains are really good at taking in a lot of information and being able to sort it and process it quickly and efficiently. The majority of children though, have not developed that skill to such a high level when they are in early years. So, when they walk into a busy space, they don't see it in the same way that we do. Their visual discrimination isn't as well honed as ours so everything tends to just become background wall paper. It is not that they have a visual impairment or the walls go all wobbly and blurry like on Scooby Doo!

It is similar to when you say to a child:

'this is an a – pple, a lovely shiny red a-pple! Listen to the sounds carefully. A-a-a-a- apple! Now then Connor, what sound can you hear at the beginning of a-pple? (bearing in mind that I have told you the answer)!'

Connor will of course answer 'c' as it is the only sound he knows. Not because it is the only sound he can hear, but he has been told that his name starts with 'c' and because his name is important to him, he remembers this.

Connor is not deaf, he is just at the early stages of developing phonological awareness. He can't yet discriminate the initial sounds in words – but he will.

It is the same with visual perception, children see it all but they don't see any of it. It becomes like wallpaper.

So, the less clutter around the space, the more impact what is actually there will have, which takes me back to my original point – if the children can see it. I know that most early years settings have not been built with the children's eye view in mind. Often their eye level is full of cupboards, sinks, trunking, units etc, which is not ideal, but you can only work with what you have got and sometimes you have to get a bit creative, repositioning your furniture and using the backs of units for display.

The setting in the photo below covered the backs of their units with ply board and painted it with blackboard paint, giving them a whole new range of working and display surfaces at child height.

I know this will sound like an April fool, but seriously, it is worth getting down onto your knees and walking/crawling around your space. It will give you a really good child's eye view of what you have got to work with. It can be equally as productive to do the same with your outdoor space as well, but get some knee pads or kneel on a skateboard and get someone else to push you round – now that is how you put the fun back into team meetings!

Once you have got your eye-level sorted out, this is where you are going to put your key teaching display. Things like phonic lines, alphabet charts, number lines etc. – all of the things that you want the children to engage with and use.

USE PHOTOGRAPHS OF THE CHILDREN

Next step is to ask yourself what are young children motivated by more than anything else? More than the latest superhero or sweets? Themselves! They are ego mad. They love nothing better than to see themselves in video or in a photo. So if we are trying to create a display that will really motivate and engage them in their learning – a display that they want to interact with and return to – what should we use in that display? You got it – them!

There are all sorts of ways that you can use children's images in display, and bearing in mind that you have just stripped all of your walls, we had better get started on exploring some possibilities. I see lots of children's creations stuck up on walls. Once the child has completed their work of art, some adult has gone through the routine of 'Oooh, that really is fantastic! Now then, do you want to take that home (where it will probably be stuck a) in a pile, b) on the fridge or c) in the bin? or do you want me to put it on our amazing 'wall of pride' where everyone in the whole world will be able to see how spectacular you are? The 'wall of pride'? Are you sure?

I wouldn't want to be seen to be influencing your decision… yes? Brilliant!'. So up it goes, with the child's name duly printed, laminated and stuck next to it which is great – apart from the fact that if I am four-years-old I might well be able to recognise my name, but I can't read so I don't know anyone else's and they don't know mine. However, if you stick my photograph up alongside my name, then everyone knows it's me and I also get the self esteem of seeing my face up on the wall.

What I usually try to do is have about half a dozen laminated photographs of each child's face and when they have done something that you or they want to put up on the wall (or wherever) I dispatch them off to get one of their photos which goes up first before their name. One setting I worked with had the photographs stuck onto pegs with the child's name underneath. This made their storage and access easy. When the child's work went up the peg was just clipped on to it wherever there was a suitable gap. It worked really well.

Another photographic initiative that I have worked on with great success is the personalised alphabet and number line. What self respecting Early Years Foundation Stage setting doesn't have a number line and alphabet frieze? It is part of the essential kit! The question really is, how many of the key children who you need to target ever independently look at your alphabet frieze or number line?

As adults we are like children in a sweet shop when it comes to these classroom essentials. There are so many to choose from. When I began my career you could only buy them from the Early Learning Centre and everyone had the same. Now, with the advent of the computer download there are literally hundreds of options.

The key is to remember who we are buying them for, and the answer is not you! They are going to be a key component that we will use every day in our work to teach children the basic skills of literacy and mathematics. There will be some children who pick up these skills relatively quickly and easily, with or without the use of the alphabet frieze and number line, but there will be others who struggle, who need a little longer to travel down their path of development. So, when it comes to considering who we are targeting with this sort of classroom display, the answer is them – the hard to reach brigade.

Bear in mind how many four-year old August-born children are really interested in and motivated by 'an apple'? Ah, but never fear because close on the heels of that stimulating fruit there is 'a ball' and then, like a gift from heaven … 'a cat'! Could there be anything less inspiring or motivational?

Sometimes, I see alphabet lines that are themed around characters that remind practitioners of their past. I saw one the other day with a very famous bear on it. The whole thing was in beautiful pastel shades of yellow. Now you would think that being a self-confessed beige lover I would be right into that. Well I'm not! The problem is, that apart from the lack of engagement for your key audience – it all looks the same! Now to our sophisticated eye, that isn't a problem but, if you are in the early stages of letter discrimination and everything is in the same font with the same background and the same style of illustrations then it makes your job of discriminating between q, o, p, a, d, b, c, and e even harder. After all, they are all just a combination of a bit of a circle that sometimes has a bit of a stick that sometimes goes up, sometimes down, sometimes left and sometimes right. It is little wonder our children get so confused!

The answer? Personalise them with children's photos. More importantly personalise key teaching displays to the children you are targeting with that knowledge – not the ones who already know it.

My name is Alistair and if you were in my class in early years, you would know that because the teacher was always shouting it out! If my teacher wanted to create a personalised alphabet, then where better to start than with me? I am going to love it and my classmates are going to be far more interested because it's not some animated apple, it's me! (Preferably sticking my tongue out for the photo as this will make the children laugh and raise the level of engagement even further!)

Make the photos nice and big. If you get to a letter of the alphabet and there is no one in your class or group whose name starts with that sound, then ask the children what they would like to put in the picture? Remember if it's an alphabet line that you are using to teach initial sounds then you can't have 'Charlotte' for 'C' or 'George' for 'G'. It has to be the sound not the name. They will come in handy later on when you start doing blends etc!

With your number line, use assessment to identify who knows what in terms of number recognition. Then create your line by targeting the children who don't know to be in the photos. Make your 'most difficult to engage child' number 1! Trust me, it works wonders.

SELF DISPLAY

Another really useful feature of display at this level is using the space to allow children to display their own work. This can be a permanent feature or something that is fairly 'organic' in that children can stick up whatever they want throughout the session/day and adults will take it down to sort, evaluate and recycle ready for the next day/session.

The idea that you can display your own work can be particularly empowering for children, especially because they are so ego driven! I am talking here about children actually displaying their own work as they finish it, probably not in consultation with an adult. This is different from adults having discussions with children about work they have produced that they are proud of and want to display in a more formal context.

These boys are in continuous provision and have been encouraged to independently mark make around their favourite obsession – football. They have to cut out the players, stick them to the sheet and then use speech bubbles to give their players a voice. Once they have done this, they can then stick their work onto the 'football display' which is well positioned and easily accessible.

As you can see it was very popular and produced some good independent work. It also gave rise to other bits of creativity like the scarf in the bottom left hand corner of this page, which once it was displayed caused a mini scarf-making craze all of its own.

This display board below has been backed and then covered with garden netting. Pegs were provided and children could easily peg up their own work.

ADULT CREATED DISPLAY FOR IMPACT

When I think back, I have wasted many hours of children's lives on pointless creation of display, whether it be scrunching up pink tissue paper to make blossom trees in spring or sprinkling sequins onto a paper plate to make a rainbow fish. The skill level has been low and the engagement of some children even lower – meaning that the learning was low.

I also quite liked the large scale, big impact display. I once did the entire nativity scene, child-sized using only the medium of tissue paper balls! It took weeks. It would be ceremoniously laid out in our 'messy area' and every day I would find myself saying 'Who would like to come and finish off a shepherd? Anyone?' By the end, my lovely teaching assistant Carole and I spent every waking minute frantically gluing tissue paper balls onto anything that moved. Who was it for? What was the learning? Who knows!

I saw this in a setting recently where they had decided to make a life-sized Ben 10 alien. They had drawn around a child in the usual CSI, dead body kind of way and then an adult had taken the outline and transformed it into the outline of an alien. This alien had a uniform on, and the uniform was to be recreated through the medium of collage, using shiny paper. Someone had spent a long time cutting up the paper and sorting it into different pots.

When it came to continuous provision, one adult said that she was going to be on the 'sticking' table doing some collage, would anyone like to join her? There was a stony silence from the room. She then did what any adult would do if they knew they had to get a life-sized Ben 10 alien collaged by the end of the day … she began fake crying! Lamenting the fact that she would be all on her own at the gluing table

with no one to help her. At this point, four girls shot their hands up and said they would join her in her sticking quest. When I got to the sticking table, Ben had been laid over it so that his torso and legs were hanging down either side of the table and all that was visible was his midriff. This was sectioned into squares with letters on that corresponded to the colour that had to be used in that square.

The girls were dutifully sticking the correct colour in the correct square using a glue stick. When I asked them why they had chosen this activity, they said it was because 'Miss was crying'! This is a classic example of a really low level activity that is not linked to learning or engagement, but is there to produce display.

Using display to engage children is a brilliant idea. If I know that I have got a group of learners that are motivated by Ben 10, then having a life-sized metallic Ben 10 in one of my areas of continuous provision is certainly going to grab their interest. But, if there is not a more productive and inspiring way of producing this display, then it should be done by an adult for children.

This is not the same as when adults work with children and 'help' them by moving their hand or adding a bit here and there, straightening up a line, chopping a bit off! This is about adults creating display for impact and engagement, giving children a bit of a 'wow' moment.

This is a superhero display created by adults around children's interests to engage them in mark-making. The windows of the sky scrapers are sticky notes which the super heroes can peel off and write messages on.

In contrast, here is an adult–created display above a sand tray. Again, who is it for? I am not sure. If you have never experienced sand before but have a higher than average reading age it might be of some use, but other than that children are not likely to look at it, and if they do they are not likely to be able to interpret or apply it. I can't help but feel that the space would be better used for something else or just left as a space, a rest for the eyes and the brain.

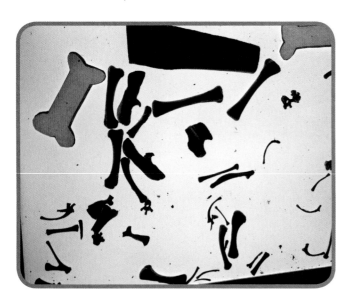

Of course, display doesn't have to be hanging on a wall. If you have got space, a low level interactive display can be great for children's engagement. I am not talking here about a collection of red things that stay on the table for a week and no one is allowed to touch! I am talking about interesting and inviting things that you want to investigate more. In the photo below, the setting has put a collection of bones onto a light box, so that the children can come and investigate the bones and make shapes.

In the above setting they used the light box again, but this time with black and clear aqua beads. The children were fascinated with how they moved on the box, the different shades and colours, but also the fact that they could see air bubbles glistening within the gel.

I have also used display as a prompt for talk, especially during snack time. Alongside the independent element of the snack area, you also want to introduce other learning opportunities. This can be as simple as having a photo or object on the table for the children to look at and talk about. As an adult moves through the learning space, they are able to drop into the snack area, re-set any of the resources that need resetting, check for loiterers and engage in a bit of quality talk.

If you are trying to encourage children to talk then you need to give them the sort of table display that they are going to want to talk about. Humour and terror (within reason) often work well as does showing them photos of past events, getting them to remember, recall, sequence and articulate their memories.

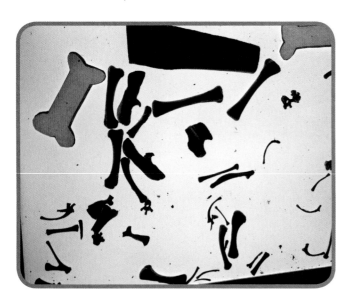

DRESSING FOR INTEREST

I first started experimenting with the concept of dressing for interests when I was looking at ways of getting children (particularly boys) to engage in a bit of mark-making. I very quickly found that even a very simple link to a particular interest could make a significant difference. Since then I have applied this concept to every area throughout the environment to see if it has the same impact, and it does! With regards to display areas, like the football display mentioned earlier, how you 'theme' the display space can really make a difference to the children who might then come and interact with it.

There is a balance though, and you need to think back to what I said about children's visual perception. You don't want to turn your space into the 'Disney shop' and fill it with cartoon clutter. When you dress for interest it should be an enhancement to your space and not a distraction. Here are some other examples of settings that have dressed display areas for interest.

Of course interest doesn't always have to be gender linked. Below is a semi-permanent display that was purely created to get children talking and thinking. It was created by adults in the outdoor space, just tucked around a corner. Its purpose was that children would discover it and then be motivated to ask questions about what it was and why was it there? Who did the crown belong to? Why was it on black fur? And so on. Adults were prepared to run with the children's ideas and use this stimulus to promote all sorts of learning opportunities.

INTERACTIVE DISPLAY

In my day it was all about flaps! That was about as interactive as you got. If you had flaps going on with your display, you were the business! These days technology allows us to add all sorts of exciting and inviting interactive elements to our display. Displays can now talk to children, ask them questions, prompt their thinking or remind them of what the display is all about. There are a huge range of 'talk' items that you can add to displays indoors and out. If you can lay your hands on talking tins, talking points, talking postcards, talking boxes, even talking pegs, they can all be used to really enhance a display space. You can even buy an interactive wall that allows you to put objects on it and then record some language around each object – hours of fun!

With the advent of the digital photograph you can also add movement to your displays with the use of digital photo frames. These can show process as well as prompt discussion and questioning.

The use of visualisers and viewers can turn your whiteboard (or wall) into an interactive display space, limited only by the resources that you have got and the children's imaginations.

Of course, the whole point of an interactive display is that you can interact with it! It is no good if it is above head (or at least stretch) height unless of course you are going to provide step ladders!

Display to celebrate achievement and attainment

For me, the next 'layer' of display is around celebrating children's achievements and building their self esteem. Making them proud of their work will make them want to produce more. But this type of display is not just about children's achievements and attainment, it is also where the staff can show their knowledge and understanding of the children in the setting, what they are currently achieving and what their next steps need to be. So, this display could be a gallery of children's work or it could be annotated by staff with some contextual statements, examples of children's voices and thoughts and some next steps.

However you do it, this display should have a context and that context should be based on learning. It is very rare that you can justify producing multiple items on a 'production line' for display these days, because that way of working is not linked to skills, it is linked to activities. Gone are the days when you would find a nice activity (often involving a hand print or a paper plate) and you would decide that everyone was going to make one. What was the purpose of this?

We should revisit my old friend 'The Rainbow Fish' as an example. Now, don't get me wrong I love the story of 'The Rainbow Fish' as have all of the children I have read it to over the years. But just because they enjoyed the story does not mean that they then want to make one out of a paper plate and some sequins! There is usually one adult who is responsible for the creation of said paper plate fish and will then dominate the 'creative' table until everyone has done them. Oh, the irony – this is the 'creative' table where children learn the skills to allow them to express their creativity in an individual and unique way, but today they can only express their creativity using the resources that I have provided: a paper plate, some glue and a few sequins, around a theme I have dictated (The Rainbow Fish), and know they have got it 'right' if it looks like mine! In this kind of activity you always start with your most compliant children first and leave the least motivated ones till last. They are the ones you will have to chase around the outdoor environment for 15 minutes before they come in! That alone should tell us something. Don't you think if they wanted to make a 'Rainbow Fish' out of a paper plate they would have done it by now?

If you have to cajole any child to come and do anything to that extent, then you can guarantee their levels of engagement are going to be low and as a result the potential of attainment is also going to be very low.

TAPPING THEIR SKILLS

During the course of your average class of 30 children you will have a huge range of interests, abilities and physical dexterity. Yet, they are all cutting a triangle out of a paper plate (low level skill) applying glue with a glue stick (lowest level skill in glue application) and then scattering some sequins on (low level dexterity skills). Only made worse if you have produced a prototype for them to copy (low level/non-existent creative development)! So why do it?

If you want to focus on children's cutting skills then does it matter what they cut? It is the cutting skill that you should differentiate. If you are looking at the skill of printing then does it matter what they print? Why does everybody have to print an Easter chick using yellow paint and half a potato? The truth is they don't. If printing is the skill you are focusing on then you should look at your children's experience of different types of printing and also the skills that are involved in being able to print.

For your more emergent printers, you might focus on printing with a range of resources with a larger surface area to make the manipulation easier. For your more advanced printer you might use objects that challenge their dexterity or encourage them to use their prior knowledge of how printing works to experiment with different ways of creating a print.

The result will not be a display of 30 potato chicks, but instead a display that clearly shows skill, process, differentiation and diversity. The diverseness of the content will show the range of interests that your children have, their skill and dexterity. Throw into that some children's voice and adult opinion and you have got yourself an attractive, high level display that shows understanding and learning and not just 30 'Rainbow Fish' that all look spookily the same!

Display to document

The third 'layer' of display is to document. If you have room then think of this 'layer' as the learning journey of your setting. I used to think that the top of my wall was for my alphabet frieze, number line and the occasional damp patch! In truth it is the least impactive of all of the display spaces that you have got indoors, but by the same token it would be a shame to waste the space.

Now, obviously this all depends on how high your ceilings are. If you are in an old Victorian building, you are likely to have oodles of room before you get to the roof, whereas in other settings you could jump up and touch the ceiling. If your space is small then keep your display focus around 'motivate' and 'celebrate'. You do not want your environment to become over cluttered.

This is going to be an opportunity for you to show and celebrate all of the great things that you have done across the year. This sort of display is a 'slow burner' starting at the beginning of the year and building slowly. It can also be a good recycler. You can use whole or partial displays that you have already made and move them. As this display is not going to be accessed by children without some support, it is a good one to annotate for other adults that may be coming into your space. This could be parents, senior management team, local authority or Ofsted. If your learning and attainment is evident on the walls then no one is going to miss anything or have to go digging for it.

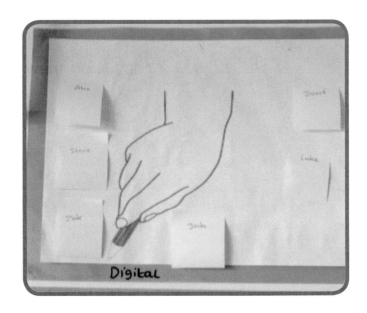

These sorts of display are really useful when you are working with children on the chronology of their year. It is good for them to revisit things that have happened in your setting and recount key events. This high level display space can also be used as a place to have visual reminders for staff.

This setting has used the space above their cupboards to have a visual reminder of where children are up to with the development of their pencil grip. The large pictures show the stages of progression and the sticky notes indicate which children are at which level. Staff can then move the sticky notes along as the children progress.

If you are going to hang displays from the ceiling it can be really effective to hang materials right down to child height. Laminate A4 photographs of children 'in action' and then attach two or three together using a hole punch and treasury tags. Hang them from the ceiling on a long thread so that the top photo hangs at children's eye line and the others go down to the floor. This way, children are far more likely to interact with them and us them as a stimulus for learning.

In this setting the team used a similar idea of low hanging images, but they copied their photos onto A4 sheets of acetate. This worked really well as it helped to maintain a more 'open' and less cluttered feel as you could see through and around the images.

In the same setting a series of twigs had been hung just above children's head height. Each twig had something different hanging down from it. There were all sorts of different pieces of work from African beads, to recycled rocket ships and wind chimes. You had to have your wits about you as an adult as you slalomed through them, but the children referenced them frequently in their play and were inspired to create things to hang from them.

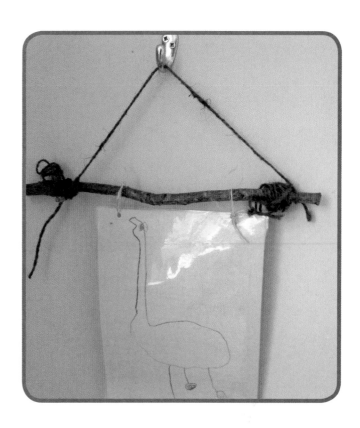

Chapter 4

Learning walls

ABC says

The basic concept of a learning wall is that each child has their own space on the wall or on a display board and different children have their work featured at different times.

The criteria for getting your work onto the wall is that it is something that you are proud of and want to display, or something that you have done really well and an adult wants to feature it. What is in the space will change over time. How regularly it changes is up to you!

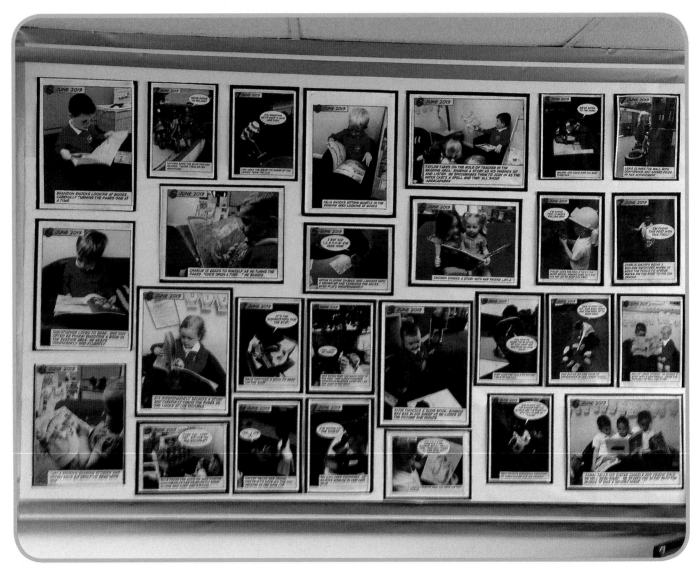

LEARNING WALLS

There are a few fundamental concepts that are worth considering with this type of display.

1. The children's work is the feature, so it shouldn't have to compete with the background.

2. A large(ish) photo of the child should always be displayed alongside their work. This links not only to children's sense of ego, but also their self esteem. 'If you display my work with my name next to it, then I know it is mine (if I recognise my name) and so do you. If you put my photograph next to it then everybody knows that it is mine.'

3. Try and give it some relevance by including some direct speech from the child, perhaps a comment on what they did or why.

4. Try adding your thoughts as a practitioner outlining some of the context around the activity. Keep it brief though. No one has time to read 'War and Peace'!

5. Consider adding some 'Next steps' statements. This not only helps to clarify the thinking of the team, but also makes it much easier to judge attainment and be aware of how learning happens in the early years, especially if you are not an early years expert.

The sort of work that appears in this type of display is often then taken down and used as evidence in learning journeys. Try and make your display work for you so that this is possible, and you don't have to create a display twice!

The photos opposite show some examples of learning walls from early years settings. They have all been interpreted slightly differently but show the range of opportunities available. In the learning wall below the practitioners have combined engagement and ICT. These photographs have been taken on a tablet and then an app has been used to turn them into a series of comic book pages. Not only does it show a 'snapshot' of the learning opportunities that exist, it is also highly motivating for the children who want to produce good work because they want their picture used for the comic book display.

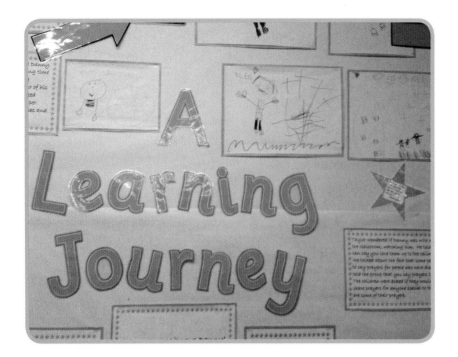

Learning stories

Learning story displays track the development of an idea or a spark of imagination, (usually that comes from the children) but then really takes off and ends up underpinning lots of your teaching and the enhancements that you put into your continuous provision. Using your display, you can then plot the different stages of how the interest developed and what other learning came from it. A child-initiated interest like this doesn't often follow the path that you think it might, and you can end up with quite an eclectic and diverse display.

This kind of display also benefits a great deal from some level of context and comment. I always try not to make these displays too small and bitty, otherwise brains don't tend to like them as there is too much to take in in a small space. It is better to keep them concise and use larger photographs and illustrations that don't overload the eyes and the brain.

If your learning story goes in a particular order then it is well worth trying to make sure that your photos and annotations follow this direction. Otherwise the whole thing won't make sense. You can even use arrows if you have the space and you think it will help!

Below is a great example of a learning story that not only shows the importance of responding to children's needs, it also highlights the randomness and resourcefulness of children! Alex has shared the news with his friends that his great grandad died. This has made him feel sad. The group are talking about ways to make people feel better when they are sad. They come up with various ingenious suggestions like pulling faces. They are then all too pleased to demonstrate their face-pulling capabilities and also telling jokes. The children then share a joke including Sam's classic 'Why did the banana go to the doctors? Because he wasn't feeling very well!' I am sure the punch line is 'because he wasn't peeling very well', but he got a laugh anyway!

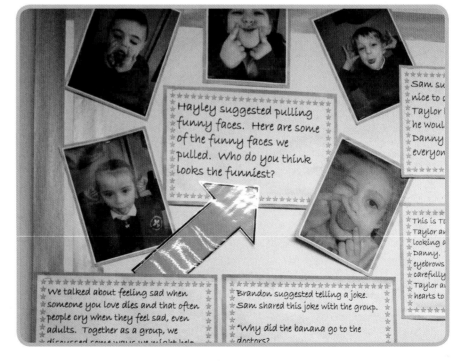

Above is another example of the same sort of display, this one is linked to Forest schools and mark-making.

Another way that you can promote talk and hopefully a bit of mark making, is to pose a 'Question of the week'. In this two-form entry reception, the question is usually linked to something topical that is affecting all of the children, like the advent of spring. The children can bring in their suggestions from home or work on them in continuous provision. The impetus for them to have a go is that their ideas will not only feature in the book, but also get displayed in this rather spectacular frame. That in itself promotes a discussion and creates an ethos of 'having a go'.

In this setting the focus was 'Angry Birds'. As you can see it is a display in progress. The idea of these displays is that you put them up whilst the interest is evolving. If the children are involved in the creation of the display and understand how it works, then they are more likely to become involved with the process and contribute to it.

There was huge diversity in the content of this display from artwork to mark-making, writing and 3D modelling. Where the adults or children have come up with a good question or problem to solve, they are written on the green question marks.

Starting with a stimulus

Display is often linked to a topic, and not just the theme of the topic but a specific activity linked to that topic. Now as I have already made very clear, I am not a fan of the 'topic' because high level attainment comes from high level engagement. To get maximum engagement for all children we need to have a diverse approach to the themes that we use in our teaching rather than just stick to one.

Assessment will tell you what the children need to know; the hardest part is capturing their interest so that they engage in the learning process and in turn the knowledge has more chance of sticking! With a 'topic' approach, not all children will be as motivated and engaged as others, so rather than giving everybody the theme of 'pirates', have a pirate focus for the children who are motivated by pirates and a different focus for the children who are motivated by something else.

In one setting I was working with, they always did a pirate topic (as you do) and part of their topic was always the discovery of a message in a bottle which the children really liked. The message in the bottle was from 'Blackbeard' and it said all sorts of piratey things like 'arrr me hearties!' and 'shiver me timbers'! The purpose of the message in a bottle was to get the children to write back to Blackbeard. So, the skill that the practitioners were trying to engage the children with was a mark-making one.

Every year the staff would make a display of the letters that the children had written back to Blackbeard. What I was interested in looking at was how the level of engagement might be higher if the children didn't have to write to Blackbeard. What if they could choose to write back to whoever they wanted?

So, the session started with the same high level stimulus – the discovery of a bottle with a message in it. But, the bottle wouldn't open so rather than be told who the message was from, the children had to guess. Guesses ranged from 'a pirate' to 'Wayne Rooney' to 'my Nana', but it didn't matter. All were equally valid. It was then suggested to the children that they wrote back to who they thought was the sender of the letter. The engagement level was high for this mark-making experience and the results were certainly diverse! The display then started with a large scale message in a bottle in the top left hand corner and all of the different responses were displayed under it. Only about five ended up being anything to do with pirates.

We have to be prepared for and encourage children to interpret the stimulus that we provide in very different ways. For some, the huge egg that you leave outside for them to find may inspire an interest in dinosaurs, but perhaps unicorns with another (who are we to say that unicorns don't hatch out of eggs?). Your planning and your teaching have to be flexible enough to allow this to happen, otherwise you are saying to children that there is only one way that they can interpret their learning … yours!

The end product of the activities that you set up should not always lead to the same outcome. The process of creating those outcomes is the important bit. What the children could produce should be applied to any theme that inspires them. Most activities should offer children the opportunity to engage in a range of processes and create lots of possibilities for open ended investigation and questioning. Our aim is always to get the children to master the skill or the process – not to get 30 versions of the same end result.

Of course, some of the activities are for inspiration to engender some of that mystical stuff known as 'awe and wonder'. These might be objects or experiences for you to create and leave for children to find or discover. Although you might have in your head what you think their response might be, be prepared to go with whatever they come up with, remembering that all of the children will probably not think the same. You can then use these objects as a starting point for display and just see what develops!

Sometimes the stimulus might come from a story or book that has really captured the children's imaginations. When this happens, you will see evidence of it not just in their enthusiasm to have the story again but also in their talk, role-play and writing.

The stimulus for this display came from the story 'Jack and the Flum Flum Tree'. Some children not only recreated their own version of a Flum Flum tree indoors, they also took their play outside and made a gigantic version. All of this was recorded on the display.

The children used the resources found outdoors to make a Flum Flum tree in the OLE. Imogen helped to push the hose pipe into the top of the drain pipe to make the branches.
Hayley and Emily then added strips of material to the branches by knotting them. They said this made the tree look more like the one from the book.

SCRAP BOOK

At Ladybrook they had a version of this in both nursery and reception. This is reception's contribution: a large display board has been divided up so that each child gets a large(ish) square.

The whole thing was really well thought out from the backing paper to the mounts that the photographs were on.

The display starts with a photo of the child and their 'significant others'. These are permanent features. The squares are then enhanced with examples of children's work and creations. Adults then annotate the work that is on display.

As this changes, the examples and the annotations could go straight into a child's learning journey as evidence. The speech bubbles record what the children were saying, so that gives a nice bit of context to the display.

This is what it looked like from a distance. There was so much information on it about learning, attainment, children's preferences and skill development. It was a very informative read.

This is the nursery version of the same idea. There were a huge variation in the creations that children had chosen to display from up-cycled models to stick art – nice!

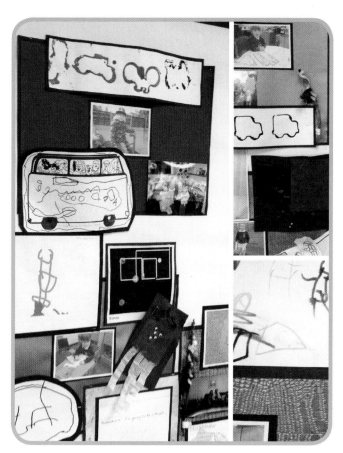

Outdoor display

Although there are shared elements of both indoor and outdoor learning, outdoors should be different as it can offer the potential for a completely different set of skills to be developed that indoors can't. Before we think about what to display outdoors and how to display it, it is worth considering what we want children to gain from outdoor experience.

★ Outdoor learning is direct

Outdoor learning can provide a dramatic contrast to the indoor classroom. Children can be far more motivated to learn outdoors as they respond to the freedom that the space offers. With good planning and preparation the outdoors can be used really effectively to engage even the most reluctant learners.

★ Outdoor learning is active

In an effective outdoor environment, children will learn through what they do, how they do it and what they discover. They are also learning new skills, and ways of thinking and working. Children have great opportunities to learn about their own preferences and levels of risk as well as interacting and working with others. As they engage in tasks they are learning skills of enquiry, experiment, feedback, reflection, review and cooperative learning to name but a few!

★ Outdoor learning is real

Outdoor learning happens in an environment where everything that children interact with and touch is natural and real. It involves the use of all of the senses and also gives children a real appreciation of cause and effect. Being outdoors can really bring learning alive.

★ Outdoor learning is stimulating

There is no limit to the experiences and curiosities that outdoor environments and activities can arouse. Children frequently surprise themselves with what they learn, not only about their environment, but about themselves and others. As outdoor learning can often be on a larger scale, it requires more physical exertion and a different way of thinking.

★ Outdoor learning is challenging

Because the outdoor environment is more subject to change as a result of the weather, the seasons and the creatures that inhabit it (including us), the outdoors can really challenge children's perceptions about why the world is the way that it is, and also challenge their thinking about how the world works and why.

★ Outdoors is continually changing

One of the really unique things about learning in the outdoors is that no two experiences will ever be the same. Even if you are working in a small space with limited resources, nature, natural inquisitiveness and exploration will ensure that space stays alive. Our role as adults is to capitalise on these changes and make sure that our children don't just look once, but go back and look again (and again)!

Whatever the weather

One of the main issues that we have with good outdoor display is the good old British weather! Whatever you create is likely to get blown about, rained on and faded by the sun (if you are lucky)! So, laminating pictures and labels and sticking them to your walls, fences and outdoor structures is ultimately going to result in a tatty, faded soggy mess!

You also need to think about the purpose of that sort of display outdoors. Who is it for? Do the children actually reference it and use it in their play and learning? Or is it just an adult-generated space filler? I would hazard a guess that it is the latter rather than the former.

I like to try and keep the majority of my outdoor display and the way that I display it as natural as possible. Using natural resources helps children to connect and explore the environment that they are working in on a much deeper level. I want my outdoor space to encourage children to think in a different way and to apply their problem solving strategies and curious tendencies in a creative and innovative way.

Although some outdoor displays that you create can be permanent, it is probably best to think of outdoor display as being semi permanent or transient. When you begin to think about it in this way, it is far easier to plan for and execute.

Transient art

We often talk about the use of 'transient art' in early years. It is one of those phrases that has become part of our regular terminology, especially with reference to the outdoor environment. The concept behind it is simple: it is art that is created but that isn't intended to be permanent – hence the term 'transient'. It can be left out in the environment but with the acknowledgement that the elements will conspire to 'deconstruct it'.

If children are going to work like this then they need to know from the beginning that they are not going to stick their creation to a piece of paper and take it home. Transient art is a great opportunity to experiment with shape and texture as well as trial and error, cause and effect. Of course, transient art can involve any resources that are not permanently fixed. It doesn't just apply to pictures, it also applies to sculpture and modelling.

In our indoor environments children get a great deal of opportunity to work with manufactured craft resources like sequins, pom poms, pipe cleaners etc. It is therefore important that when you are thinking about transient art outdoors that you use natural materials. This way children get to experience and handle first-hand some objects that they will have just looked at, or maybe never seen before.

They also have to use their creativity to take an object out of its 'usual' or 'natural' context and use it to create something unique or as a substitute for something else, so a fir cone could be part of a natural sculpture, but it could also be used as the head of a woodland creature or to represent a hedgehog.

USEFUL NATURAL RESOURCES

- large stones
- pebbles
- gravel
- fir cones
- conkers
- nuts
- seeds
- leaves
- leaf veins
- sticks and twigs
- twine
- glass beads
- peas
- beans
- pulses
- petals

- glass beads
- coffee beans
- feathers
- log slices
- moss
- moss balls
- wicker balls
- bark
- logs
- bamboo
- wool
- shells
- sponge
- mopami wood

- glass beads
- gem stones (like fluorspar)
- sand (black and golden)
- agates
- coconut shells
- yellow beans
- buddha nuts
- drift wood
- talami
- mintola
- large lingzhi
- dried limes
- dried oranges

This is by no means an exhaustive list, but will certainly get you started. Obviously, check small items for their potential choking hazard and also that any dried seed heads and pods are non-toxic.

One thing that can be really useful to help children with their transient artwork is to give them a 'frame' to work within or a 'canvas' to work on. You can easily create different sized frames from twigs which you can either glue together or bind together in the corners with string or raffia. Once these are made you can use them again and again. The variety of sizes allows children to either select a frame to work within or one to frame their finished work.

Outdoor display is no different to indoor display in that it should have a purpose and be created for impact, engagement (to teach a skill) or celebration. It just won't manifest itself on a display board. It is likely to be part of the environment and will often be transient. There is huge amount of scope and interpretation when it comes to displaying outdoors, and often it is the activity that the children are engaging in that becomes the display. You don't have to take it away, back it and mount it!

Here are some ideas and inspirations for outdoor display; they are only intended as a starting point and not the end result!

When it comes to other ways to make a frame then a paving stone is a very useful thing to have around. I know that paving stones have gone out of fashion a bit when it comes to designing outdoor spaces, but they can be a great addition to your setting.

If you want to provide a canvas, as opposed to a frame, then anything that is portable and a manageable size for children will do. In the past I have used pillow cases (these are great because they roll up and are washable), carpet squares (the great thing about these is that the pile of the carpet can help the resources that the children are creating with stay in place), and ceramic or slate floor tiles (these can be heavier than the others and will break if they are dropped, but they often add another dimension in terms of texture).

Your environment on display

WHAT'S THE IDEA?

This is about literally putting your outdoor environment in the frame. I have used the idea below to encourage children to really look closely at a space that they may well see every day. You can also use it as an invitation for the children to recreate or interpret what they see by providing art resources.

As I said earlier in the book, with regard to indoor display, children rarely look up unless prompted to do so. Whereas indoors there is not a great deal to see up there (other than the odd damp patch!), outdoors there can be lots to look at.

WHAT DO I NEED?

You are going to be making frames that you can lean up against outdoor objects like a tree, brickwork or stone or frames that you can push into the ground or hang.

To make your own frames you just need sticks of different sizes. For each frame you need two long sticks and two short sticks. If you are pushing your frames into the ground make sure that you leave enough length on your two long sides. You can glue or stick your frames together

If you don't want to make stick frames, you can use conventional picture frames with the glass taken out. They are not as natural, but they can have real impact.

HOW DOES IT WORK?

Find points of interest in your outdoor space. Don't forget to look up as well as down. Position frames in front of the areas you have identified. If you want to encourage the children's creativity, provide a selection of materials that will support them to interpret what they see. If you framed a daffodil, don't just put out green and yellow resources. The children might not see a daffodil in the same way that you do and they might be more interested in drawing the spider they can see on the ground next to it!

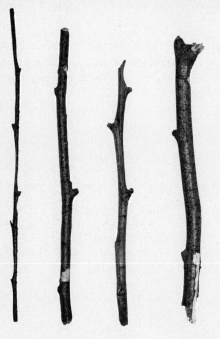

Put it in a jar

WHAT'S THE IDEA?

To be honest it doesn't have to be a jar, just something clear so that the children can see into it. In the past I have made these with empty 1 litre fizzy drinks bottles with the label removed (just cut the bottle in two about a third of the way down). You want the children to look at aspects of their outdoor environment from a different angle and also see how things look on their own and en masse.

WHAT DO I NEED?

Any clear vessel will do. Different sizes and shapes are always interesting as they can alter and distort the image that the children see. You then need things to put into your 'vessels'. You can either create these collections for or with the children, or let them collect on their own. You want the children to be able to observe them at eye level so you may need a handy table, log or wall to stand them on.

HOW DOES IT WORK?

The children have the opportunity and time to observe elements of their environment in a unique way. You might want to provide resources like magnifying glasses and mark-making materials. The children often want to touch and move the objects in the containers; I would encourage this. You can also completely change the view they have by adding water.

Hitting the tiles

WHAT'S THE IDEA?

You are going to space these tiles out around your outdoor space to encourage the children to create a piece of transient art. Don't forget to place them at different heights and in different space where the light will be different.

WHAT DO I NEED?

I would use a variety of ceramic, stone or slate tiles in a range of sizes. If you are keeping your display natural in its feel, go for a plain tile in a neutral colour (or black) rather than something brightly coloured. You will also need to provide a variety of natural resources for the children to use or let them forage their own from your outdoor space.

HOW DOES IT WORK?

The children will use found or given natural resources to create a picture or sculpture on their tile. You can then photograph the finished result as a memento.

Hanging about

WHAT'S THE IDEA?

As you are probably lacking walls and display boards outside, you are going to use what you have got to frame and display children's work. The frames can be a permanent feature but the artwork will appear in themtemporarily and then move inside lest it get rained on and ruined. The hanging frames are a really good incentive for children to produce some great outdoor work.

WHAT DO I NEED?

You need a selection of frames in a range of sizes. These can either be made or bought. You will also need plenty of string or natural yarn for hanging them, and if you are hanging your frames from a tree, you need to ensure that you have followed all of the appropriate guidelines for working up a ladder and remain safe at all times!

HOW DOES IT WORK?

The children will produce work which you can then attach with sticky tack into the frame for everyone to see. Make sure that your frames are low enough for you to be able to do this without needing a ladder every time.

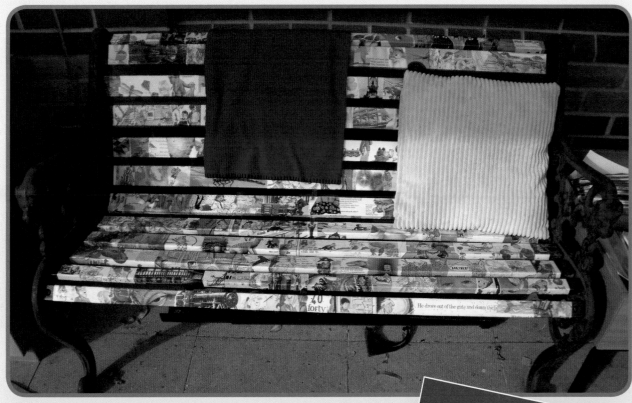

Bench makeover

WHAT'S THE IDEA?

Use children's artwork and a bit of varnish to make an old bench look splendid.

WHAT DO I NEED?

You need a collection of children's artwork inspired by the outdoors and also photographs of the children using the space as well as any other creations that they have made. You need some scissors for cutting and some PVA glue for gluing. When your bench is finished, you are going to need to weather proof it so you will need to give it a couple of coats of outdoor varnish.

HOW DOES IT WORK?

Cut up the resources that you have collected to a manageable size and glue them onto the bench with your PVA glue. When the bench is full and the glue is dry then give it a couple of coats of varnish. Your bench has now become a visual reminder of all of the great creativity that goes on in your outdoor space. If you use photographs, photocopy them onto paper first. It makes them much easier to apply!

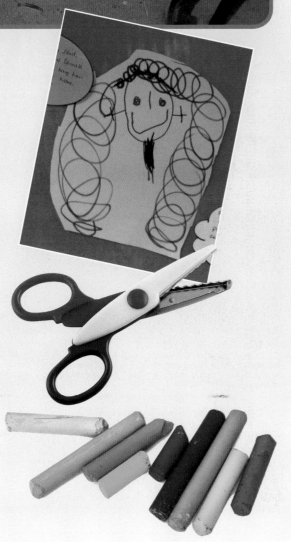

Construction sculptures

WHAT'S THE IDEA?

This is a very simple idea that combines children's love of construction with the concept of sculpture. The children are going to use natural materials or a construction kit made from natural materials to create a unique outdoor structure.

WHAT DO I NEED?

Use a wooden construction kit if you have one; if not, the children can use sticks of various sizes, log slices and other natural materials. You can either provide these or encourage the children to forage for them themselves.

HOW DOES IT WORK?

Not only will children be exploring and consolidating their construction skills, they will also be creating art through sculpture. I often find that these structures become the focus for small world play. They can be a continuous feature of your outdoor space if the children's interest is there, especially if you have introduced a fantasy concept like fairies at the bottom of the garden. (More on that later.)

Tree, stick or rock wrapping

WHAT'S THE IDEA?

The children (with some support from you) are going to use fabric, wool, ribbon etc. in blocks of colour or pattern to wrap the trunks and branches of trees – or sticks and rocks if you haven't got a tree! Once again, they are using familiar resources in an unfamiliar way to create art. This will help children not only to engage with the texture and the colour of the wrapping but also the texture and properties of the thing that they are wrapping.

WHAT DO I NEED?

I have wrapped trees in all sorts of things from bed sheets to saris, depending on what is available. Old wool and chiffon scarves work well. I have also wrapped trees in fabric that the children have printed on first. This needs to be done with fabric dye otherwise it will run when it rains. You can also wrap your tree in plain fabric like cotton or calico and then paint it when it is in situ. Some safety pins will come in very handy to fix items in place.

HOW DOES IT WORK?

This sort of display has high level visual impact because of the sheer size of it. It gives you lots of opportunity to talk

to the children about scale, texture and colour. Usually you would start at the bottom of the tree and work your way up, pinning, pegging or tying the fabric as you go. If you are going to get the children to paint the fabric once it is in situ, it can be quite laborious with a small paint brush, so you might want to consider using large sponges for printing, splatter painting or even wet tea bag flinging (dip them in paint first!).

Curiosity boxes

WHAT'S THE IDEA?

These wall mounted or floor standing boxes give children the opportunity to create transient 3D art or sculpture within a defined space. The box will help to protect their work from the elements but also allow them to revisit it to make changes. It also encourages interactive and collaborative work between children.

WHAT DO I NEED?

Ideally you need a wooden box, like a fruit box or apple crate. A cardboard box will do the job but will need replacing on a fairly regular basis. If you are going to mount your wooden boxes on the wall, then you will need the appropriate equipment (or site manager) to do that. Make sure that you mount them at children's eye height, otherwise they might have a bit of a stretch!

HOW DOES IT WORK?

I would usually give the children free access to the outdoor environment plus any of the resources that I have available. If you have a box with handles, slits or gaps in it, they can use these for pushing in fabric, grass, sticks – whatever they can find.

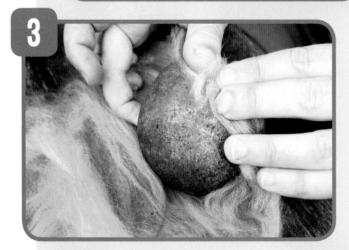

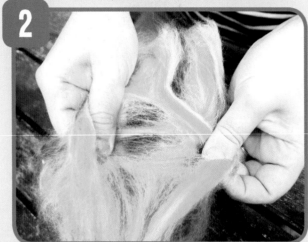

Felted stone stack

WHAT'S THE IDEA?

Felting is a relatively simple process that very young children can quickly get the hang of. Once the children have learned to felt their stones then you can use this combination of two natural materials (stone and wool) in all of your transient art and outdoor sculpture. They are also great for small world play enhancement.

WHAT DO I NEED?

You need stones and pebbles of different sizes. I have felted some really large stones, which worked well, but you need to be able to lift them and manoeuvre them – so no boulders!

You also need to buy some wool roving (see the photo). Make sure that the children can access an old clean towel, a bowl, some washing up liquid and a plastic bag (under supervision of course).

I let the children have a bowl of warm water and access to a water supply, but if you haven't got a water butt or an outdoor tap, they will need some cold water.

HOW DOES IT WORK?

Basically, you pull out your roving (the children really like this bit) smoothing it out all of the time. For a good felt it is worth doing a few layers. I have discovered that it works even better if each layer is perpendicular to the last one. It should be wider and about three times longer than the chosen stone. Then you put the stone on top of the roving and wrap it up. Be careful to tuck in the ends as you go (the children will need help with this if it is their first try).

Hold the fuzzy stone in your hand and splash it with warm water with a couple of squirts of washing up liquid in it. Then you pass your wet, woolly creation between your hands (as if you are playing catch) – this is why you can't do it easily with a boulder! Keep adding more warm water and a bit more soap if you need it and keep moving the stone between your hands, gently rubbing it until the fibres start to really knit together.

For the last part of the process you dunk your now felty rock into cold water and then transfer it into your plastic bag. Rub the stone from the outside of the bag until the fibres are nice and tight. If you get holes or the wool falls off then either your roving wasn't thick enough or you didn't work it for long enough in the warm water stage! Then you leave the stones to dry.

Tyre art

WHAT'S THE IDEA?

Although tyres these days are not made from natural rubber and so are therefore more than a little removed from the 'natural' feel of the outdoors, they are used a great deal in our outdoor environments and therefore lend themselves to creativity and display. You can work on them if they are flat on the ground, but also across and inside them if they are hanging up.

A series of tyres hanging up, some with artwork within them and some that are planted can make a high impact display.

WHAT DO I NEED?

Tyres! Make sure that they are clean and free of sharp objects. To decorate your tyres you can use a variety of resources from paint to fabric. It will just depend what interests the children. If you are going to hang them then you will need strong rope and any appropriate fixings.

HOW DOES IT WORK?

If you want to paint your tyres then it is a really good tip to prime them first with a spray paint primer which helps the paint to stick. You can then use any outdoor paint to cover your tyre. Many outdoor paints are oil based, so if the children are going to have a go make sure they are well covered and you have something appropriate to wash their hands in afterwards.

If you are going to wrap your tyre then you need lots of strips of fabric, ribbon or wool. You just keep wrapping until you can't see any more tyre!

Mirror work

WHAT'S THE IDEA?

Working on a mirror or mirrored plastic can help children to experience the outdoor environment in a whole new way. A mirror laid flat under a tree allows the children to see inside the canopy at the same time as they are looking at the roots.

When there are building and creating, the mirror image of their work means that it takes on a whole new dimension which can support their creative development. Children can also paint directly onto mirror (use thick paint with a squirt of PVA glue in it) to represent what they see or to enhance the mirror image.

WHAT DO I NEED?

A selection of mirrors or mirrored plastic sheet in a range of sizes. (Make sure you have an appropriate risk assessment in place for real mirrors.) Lots of transient art materials, paint, brushes and sponges, natural construction kits. Include a camera so they can take photos of their masterpieces.

HOW DOES IT WORK?

You can lay your mirror or mirrored plastic sheet on the ground and let the children create pieces of transient art or model make on it. Place your mirrors in unusual locations that will give your children a view of an object or space that they have never had before. Provide creative resources that will allow the children to record and interpret what they have seen.

Clay faces

WHAT'S THE IDEA?

The children can make a display of their own or anyone else's face using clay and natural materials. If you haven't got clay or it is too stiff for the children to work, this works equally as well with play dough. I just usually add a bit of sand or soil into my mix to give it a bit of texture. The faces can be created on any surface where they will stick, like a wall or a tree trunk. En masse, they make a really high impact outdoor display and are a nice alternative or enhancement to the painted portrait that often adorns the indoor display.

WHAT DO I NEED?

A block of clay or a batch of play dough is a good starting point. When your modelling medium is at the right consistency, try mixing in a variety of other things to give it texture. Lots of small natural materials for features.

HOW DOES IT WORK?

Before they can create models of their faces, the children will have to be aware of what their own face looks like. It is important that the children appreciate that this is only a representation of their face and that they might not necessarily be able to find something that will give them blue eyes or blonde hair. Having said that, children are often very resourceful in their foraging and usually manage to find something that will do!

Puddle art

WHAT'S THE IDEA?

Here, you want children to create a wet but colourful display based around experimenting with colour in puddles. Everything acts differently when it is wet, so the children will be able to observe lots of change as well as have the opportunity to explore their creativity.

WHAT DO I NEED?

A puddle! Some oil, food colouring, small bowls and sheets of paper or dried leaves. You can also do this activity with powder paint, in which case you can do all of the above, but just substitute the food colouring for powder paint and miss out the oil.

HOW DOES IT WORK?

Put a few teaspoons of oil into several different small containers. Then add three or four drops of food colouring to each container (just use one colour per container). Then you need to mix really quickly until the food colouring separates into little droplets within the oil. When you are ready, you tip the food colouring and oil mixtures onto the surface of your puddle (you have to be a bit quick here or the food colouring and oil combination begins to sink).

As soon as you have tipped your last pot, lay a sheet of paper on the top of the puddle and leave it there until you can start to see the colour faintly coming through the back. Then lift it off the puddle and hey presto! If you are using powder paint then just shake different colours onto the surface of the puddle and lay your paper on. This works just as well in a shallow puddle (sometimes better) or on wet tarmac.

Foil rubbing

WHAT'S THE IDEA?

The children are going to use the foil to help them to look at objects in a different and unique way. Not only will there be lots of opportunities for discussion about what they are seeing, there will also be opportunities to talk about texture and form.

WHAT DO I NEED?

Tin foil and a pair of scissors.

HOW DOES IT WORK?

The children take different-sized pieces of tin foil and find textures and surfaces that they think look interesting and would make a good rubbing. There is often a bit of trial and error when they first start, as anything that is too bumpy or spikey will rip the tin foil and anything that is too smooth won't leave a pattern. Once they have made a good rubbing they can bring them all to be displayed in one central space like a tree trunk or wall. Alternatively, you can attach the foil pieces directly next to the image they represent or you can even attach them to thread/string and hang then from trees or shrubs.

Collecting sticks

WHAT'S THE IDEA?

Children love to forage and collect in the outdoors – so much so that they often run out of hands and pockets to put their collections in! If they use a collecting stick they not only have somewhere to put what they find but the stick itself becomes a ready-made display.

WHAT DO I NEED?

Ideally, you need to be on the lookout for sticks with a 'V' shape at the end (like a large catapult) and a handle to hold. If you can't find any of these you will have to experiment with joining two sticks together. You also need lots of string, ribbon or wool.

HOW DOES IT WORK?

You are going to create a 'mesh' in the 'V' shape of your stick by winding your wool, string or twine backwards and forward. Start at the top of one side of your 'V' and then work your way down to the bottom. On larger sticks there will be more than enough room to come back up to the top again.

Once you think your 'V' is full enough, tie off your wool string or twine. You then take your stick with you when you go collecting and anything you find you tuck or weave in between the strings. You can then stand the sticks against a wall or tree on their own or in a group.

Ice art

WHAT'S THE IDEA?

To use ice as a medium to explore and display children's work in the outdoor environment. You can create ice displays for the children to encourage them to look closely at the objects you have encased in ice, and you can also encourage the children to make their own individual or group projects.

WHAT DO I NEED?

You need a number of shallow containers, some water and lots of natural resources. Oh, and of course a freezer, unless you are doing this activity in the depths of winter when it might be cold enough for the water to freeze on its own overnight.

HOW DOES IT WORK?

First you need to select the container that you are going to work in and then the things that you would like to freeze in it. Put a small amount of water in the bottom of your container first, otherwise if you arrange the resources in the bottom first, when you pour on the water they all move about (very annoying)!

You will probably want to hang them up when they are frozen so make sure that you dangle a piece of string, wool or twine into the water before you freeze it. When they are frozen turn them out. If you are displaying them individually then you can tie them directly onto your tree or bush.

If you are making 'ice bunting' then you can tie your ice art onto a longer piece of string. In the winter these pieces of art will last for a long time; in the summer they are a very beautiful but brief display.

Fairy folk

WHAT'S THE IDEA?

This is an adult-generated outdoor display to provoke a response from the children. It has numerous links to every aspect of the curriculum but can be particularly useful for supporting children in being creative and critical thinkers. You are going to create a 'fairy scene' in your outdoor space that will make the children think that you have fairies living in your environment.

WHAT DO I NEED?

Lots of miniature or dolls house resources as well as a range of small natural materials that the fairies might use. Let your imagination go to town!

HOW DOES IT WORK?

You need to find a secluded space to set up your fairy 'scene'. Try and keep it as open ended as possible. When the children discover what you have created, let them tell you what they think the fairies do, look like and need rather than you telling them.

You want the children to then engage in creating 'things' for the fairies using the natural materials they have to hand. This could be clothing, shelter, a bridge, musical instruments – the list is endless!

They can then add to and extend this display over long periods of time, with a little surreptitious support from you on behalf of their fairy friends. Some have lasted an entire year and ended up as more of a fairy kingdom!

Stick art

WHAT'S THE IDEA?

In creating this display, you are getting the children to look at familiar objects in a different way and explore their creativity. The children are going to first collect their sticks and then paint them. Once they are painted, you can stack them or drive them into the ground to create a stick sculpture.

WHAT DO I NEED?

Lots of sticks of different sizes and lots of paint. If you are going to leave them outside then you will need to varnish the finished product. As an altenative to paint, you can also bind your sticks in wool, ribbon or fabric. You can also add beads or various other natural materials – whatever takes the children's fancy.

HOW DOES IT WORK?

If you are painting your sticks, spend some time talking to the children about the different shapes, pits, holes and knobbly bits that they can see on their stick. If the stick is large then you might want to paint with a sponge to start with and then fill in more detail with a smaller brush later. If your sticks are smaller then you can always stand them up in a plant pot full of sand or soil. If you are going to wrap your sticks then you need a variety of yarns and string. Try to keep it as natural as possible.

Tree art

WHAT'S THE IDEA?

Did you know that trees and bushes can draw? Well, they can with a little bit of help from us! The children will be exploring different sorts of mark-making media as well as some basic science and a bit of weather. They can then use their creative streaks to enhance the marks that the tree has created by adding their own. This tree art can then be displayed around the trunks of the trees.

WHAT DO I NEED?

Depending on what sort of tree or bush you choose, you might need a range or resources. You are going to be attaching felt tips to your greenery so I would take along some felt tips, some elastic bands, sticky tape, pegs and string. You also need some large pieces of paper, like lining paper.

HOW DOES IT WORK?

You want to attach your felt tips to the ends of the twigs or branches of your tree or bush. Once the felt tip is attached, its tip should just be touching the ground. If you are working with a small shrub or a tree like a weeping willow whose leaves touch the ground, then you can just peg or elastic band the felt tips on. If your branch is a bit higher, then you might need to use sticky tape to fix your felt tip to a piece of string and then suspend it from the tree. Put a piece of paper under the felt tips and wait for a breeze. As the tree moves in the wind it will create a picture. It is quite mesmerising to watch.

Miniature forest

WHAT'S THE IDEA?

Well, the basic idea for this came from the fact that trees are very tall and early years children are very small. This can cause some considerable issues when it comes to them accessing outdoor display. Also some settings don't have a tree or room for one. So, if we could create some sort of portable miniature tree then this would be a really good addition to an early years outdoors (and indoors) setting.

WHAT DO I NEED?

A friendly tree surgeon is a good start but not essential. You are looking to collect some large(ish) tree branches that you can strip the lower twigs off to create a trunk.

Once you have got your mini tree ready, you can then either plant it directly into the ground using post cement, stand it upright in a bucket and fill the bucket with cement to keep it upright, or you can do what I have done and put the trunk into a slice of wood, as is sometimes done with a Christmas tree.

HOW DOES IT WORK?

Well, the scope for using these is endless. You can hang things from them or between them. You can use them for weaving, display children's work within them or use them to create defined areas in your indoor and outdoor space. What is great about them is that they are portable, natural and make a very effective display.

Outdoor loom

WHAT'S THE IDEA?

This is really just another version of weaving, but it is one that can stay outdoors and that children can revisit again and again. It can be made in various sizes. A good mixture of sizes makes a really good display.

WHAT DO I NEED?

You need a collection of plant pots from small to large. Terracotta are the most stable, so if you use plastic then you will have to fill the base with some pebbles or stones. You need some good stiff card, corrugated is best. A pair of scissors and several sticks or withies. Lots of materials to weave with.

HOW DOES IT WORK?

You draw around the top of your plant pot onto a piece of corrugated cardboard and cut that out. You are going to push that piece of card into the top of your pot, so you want it to be a good tight fit. Before you put the card into the pot, place it on a soft surface (like grass) and use your scissors to make holes around the edge of your circle.

If your pot is big, you will need more holes, if it is small you will only need a few. Just make sure that the holes are not too near the edge or your card will rip. Once you have made your holes (adults should do this), push the card into the top of the plant pot, making sure it is nice and secure. Then take your sticks or withies and push them into the holes so that they stand up straight.

You are now ready to weave. Start at the bottom and work your way up using a variety of textures. You can add in the odd object here and there if that takes your fancy.

Final word

There is not enough space in one book to show every sort of display that you might want to create in your setting, but what I hope that I have done here is to outline some of the thoughts and principles that should underpin the displays that you create.

★ There should be a clear link to assessment, skill and diversity and not just activity. You should always carry the mantra 'What is it and who is it for?' in your head. If you can't answer this then that probably means it is not an effective display.

★ When it comes to outdoors, treat it like outdoors and not indoors taken outside. Celebrate its uniqueness and reflect the differences in the displays you create.

Most of all, I might have said that display can benefit from being neutral, but no one said it has to be dull.

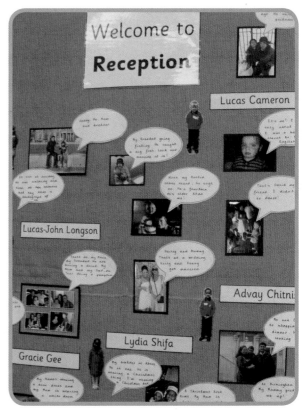

ABC says

Remember – less is more, not less is morgue!